RAY DIO
RYTERSKI

WE, WHO WALKED BENEATH THE STARS

POEMS

UNIVERSITY PRESS

OF THE SOUTH

2023

Copyright 2023 by Ray Dio Ryterski.

All rights reserved. No part of this publication may be reproduced, stored in a retrieval system, or transmitted, in any form or by any means, electronic, mechanical, photocopying, recording or otherwise, without the prior written permission of the Publisher.
Published in the United States by The University Press of the South. Printed in France by Bookmundo .

E-mail: universitypresssouth@gmail.com
Visit our award-winning web pages: www.unprsouth.com
www.punouveaumonde.com

.
We, Who Walked Beneath The Stars. Poems.
Foreword by Ethan Lewis.
First English Edition. Poetry Series, 42.

54 pages.
Front Cover Art: 'Starry Night' (KJ Pargeter, Freepik).
Front Cover Design by Stan Levêque. Reproduced with Permission.

1. Literature. 2. Poetry. 3. USA. 4. Illinois. 5. Poetry Contest. 6. Inaccessible Origins. 7. Enactment. 8. Logopoeia. 9. Ethan Lewis. 10. Ray Dio Ryterski.

ISBN: 978-1-952799-51-8
2023

To my readers, whoever, wherever, and however you may be

Table of Contents

In Lieu of Foreword: Unconventional Fore-Words on an Unconventional Poet   7
-Ethan Lewis

1. In The Beginning   13
2. We, Who Walked Beneath The Stars   15
3. These Hands   17
4. Doppelgänger Inside My Bedroom Mirror   19
5. Wall Décor   21
6. Unopened Doll   23
7. Terracotta   25
8. Rest Your Mind   27
9. To The Place Where The Black Sea Ends   29
10. Somewhere, Anywhere, A Train Runs Through It   31
11. Day & Age, Sam's Town, & Me   33
12. Pavane Pour Une Infante Defunte   35
13. The Night We All Sang Together   37
14. What We Must Do   39
15. What We Haven't Fixed   41
16. Thinking Of You   43
17. All That Have Fallen   45
18. Face The Curtain   47
19. In The Apocalypse   49
20. We, Who Stood Upon The Earth   51

In Lieu of Foreword:
Unconventional Fore-Words on an Unconventional Poet

"A poem is a walk," wrote A.R. Ammons.[1] Ray Ryterski's poems confirm that credo. The long and winding lines (justified on the right margin, as in prose, though often effectively, and *conscientiously* enjambing) unwind as peripatetic meditations. You will not find solutions in this work. (No surprise: few poets presume—and still fewer should presume—to problem-solve.) You will often encounter despair (as heart-wrenching, as shocking, as Plath's or Sexton's). But despite that despondency, and always (which is why I'm wagering that this poet pushes past a premature demise), you will be presented with Ryterski persevering.

> And so we get up and continue walking where our feet guide us
> And then one day leads to another day and another and another
> Like trying to hold sand, the time slips out from between our fingers

In fact, though, Ryterski's wanderings yield tangible destinations[2], generated *in* and *by* their movement. As nearly put in the poem just cited, the eponymous "We, Who Walked Beneath the Stars":

> I was looking for something that was absent but was set down
> I knew for a fact that the thing was lying around here somewhere

To gloss the modus operandi, tweak the lines a bit: 'I was looking for something that was absent *but about to be set down* / I knew for a fact that the thing was lying around *en route*.' In trying to explicate Ryterski's process, I similarly sought something absent yet set down, which I knew for a fact lay somewhere in my library. But where? Ah! *the prose style of Ryterski's poems* (as distinct from a style of prose; i.e., Ryterski's pieces read as poems, "language charged with meaning" [Pound[3]]) jogged my memory to Morris Croll's observation on such seventeenth century prose masters as Burton, Bacon, Browne:

> Their purpose was to portray, not a thought, but a mind thinking, or, in Pascal's words, *la peinture de la pensée*. They knew that an idea separated from the act of experiencing it is not the idea that was experienced. The ardor of its conception

in the mind is a necessary part of its truth; and unless it can be conveyed to another mind in something of the form of its occurrence, either it has changed into some other idea or it has ceased to be an idea, to have any existence whatever except a verbal one. [They] chose as the moment of expression that in which the idea first objectifies itself in the mind, in which, therefore, each of its parts still preserves its own peculiar emphasis and an independent vigor of its own—in brief, the moment in which truth is still *imagined*.[4]

Numbering among those truths-imagined-in-the-moment by Ryterski, "In the Beginning," in multiple senses of that phrase.—I.e., the first pair of poems, that so titled and "We, Who Walk Beneath the Stars," instance a preoccupation with inaccessible origins[5]:

I try to think of who the very first person was, but for every person that has existed
There is another person that has come before them so no one will ever know who
The original first person was because even the original first has an ancestor, correct

…

It still feels like we're taking the first step; we try to remember when
We took the first step, but for every step one takes there is another
Someone took before, so we'll never know who took the original first[6]

The second conceptualization recalls Seamus Heaney in "Bogland":

Our pioneers keep striking
Inwards and downwards

Every layer they strip
Seems camped on before.[7]

When the last word ambiguously resonates between adverb and noun—such that in effect, there is no last word, rather a vertiginous *enactment* as well as expression of *en abyme*. Which segues to remarking Ryterski's own brand of word-play. In "Hands," for instance:

> It's funny how your hands can do so much and so little simultaneously
> My hands can help me type this poem and drink my third cup of coffee
> They can help me carry my things and shove favorite foods into my face
> But when push comes to shove, I can't seem to get my hands dirty with
> The meaningful, impactful work that really needs to be done in the world

Logopoeia, or "the dance of the intellect with words" (both Poundisms[8]) is displayed with remarkable felicity in moving forth and back upon literal and figurative linguistic registers ("Hands can help me shove…/push comes to shove/I can't seem to get my hands dirty.")[9] Also characteristic of particular craft, refreshingly irreverent diction. With "shove favorite foods into my face," cf. "I'm done with this fuckery." "Doppelganger In My Bedroom Mirror," whence that last locution derives, points up a further facet for appreciation.

Ryterski will always prompt thought—better put, *provoke* reflection. Which revision on my part goes so far as to say that the musings this poet generates often trouble the reader. Does so doing prove analogous to the plausible conduct of Ray Ryterski's "Doppelganger"? (Is it, to some degree, a mirror image of each our own doppelgangers?)

> I told my therapist at the time about how there's a doppelganger following me
> "What if the doppelganger is trying to help you in some way?," they asked
> "I don't think so. If they were trying to help me, they wouldn't cause me pain."
> "Well, Ray, sometimes the parts of us that cause us pain are trying to help us,
> But somehow go too far. Maybe this part of you just went too far in helping you."

This poem concludes on a twist reminiscent of that author—which author? "Borges, [or] the other one,"(?) whose—whose?—meditation concludes, "I am not sure which of us it is that's writing this page."[10] Similarly,

> So when you see me in the real world, who do you see walking around as me?
> Is who you see the real me, or is the person you see the person from the mirror?

We can read the last line, hinging on "or," appositively—"the real me" *as* "the person from the mirror"—with our interpretation abetted by construing "from the mirror" in reference (also) to the person once before the glass who stepped away "from" it when venturing "in[to] the real world." Yet, typically, Ryterski's own words reflect (*mot juste!*) our feelings, in this case of being haunted by ourselves.[11] Though, to pivot on the analogy of doubles posited above, I don't think these poems "go too far…in helping us." Rather, they test, and attest to, the poet's and reader's respective resolve.

-Ethan Lewis
Springfield, Illinois, 2023

Notes

1.) Ammons titled his 1967 essay thus.
2.) This posited locus accessible through perseverance is more emphatically remarked (though the precise terminus remains ambiguous) in two remarkable poems of transit, "To the Place Where the Black Sea Ends" and "Somewhere, Anywhere, A Train Runs Through It." Cf. also the resolve expressed at the close of "What We Must Do" and of "What We Haven't Fixed."
3.) Cf. "How to Read" (1921), *Literary Essays of Ezra Pound*, ed. T.S. Eliot (New York: New Directions, 1968); Pound, *ABC of Reading* (New York: New Directions, 1935), 28. Pound compasses all "literature" within that definition. Hence in retrospect, if one preferred to categorize Ryterski's writings as prose, certainly they could. Yet I shall refer to them as poetry, due to their rhythm, lineation, and as distinct from being *prosaic*.
4.) Morris W. Croll, "The Baroque Style in Prose" [1929; rpt. In] Alexander Witherspoon and Frank J. Warnke, eds. *Seventeenth-Century Prose and Poetry* (New Haven: Yale UP, 1982), 1066.
5.) Ryterski rings variations on this concern in "Wall Décor" and "Terracotta."
6.) Acknowledging what one can't know much less return to evinces frustration in these poems, but with respect to that perseverence I've remarked, likewise spurs Ryterski forward. The poet intuits that "one person who started it all, starpower swirling in between their palms…. I want desperately to be like them, to live and to love like they do…What starpower do I hold? What do I have to offer? / Instead of holding the universe I am standing on shaky ground

that isn't mine;… / But I can write a poem or two, so that is where I find myself in my own tiny beginning."

7.) Seamus Heaney, *Selected Poems 1966-1987* (New York: Farrar Straus Giroux, 1990), 22-3.

8.) "*Logopoeia*, 'the dance of the intellect with words, that is to say, it employs words not only for their direct meaning, but it takes count in a special way of habits of usage, of the context we *expect* to find with the word, its usual concomitants, of its known acceptances, and of ironical play. It holds the aesthetic content which is peculiarly the domain of verbal manifestation, and cannot possibly be contained in plastic or music. It is the latest come, and perhaps the most tricky and undependable mode [as distinct from *phanopoeia*, "a casting of images upon the visual imagination," and *melopoeia*, "wherein the words are charged, over and above their plain meaning, with some musical property, which directs the bearing or trend of that meaning"]." ("How to Read," 25)

9.) Cf. a similar, though more dire, shuttling in "Face the Curtain": "I can't kill myself for the life of me; for the life of me, something's holding me back."

10.) Cf. "Borges y Yo" ("Borges and I"), Jorge Luis Borges, *Collected Fictions*, trans. Andrew Hurley (New York: Penguin, 1998), 324; Borges, *Collected Poems*, ed. Alexander Coleman, trans. Kenneth Krabbenhoft, et al. (New York: Penguin, 1999), 92-3.

11.) As in, e.g., "Wall Décor," which in the process of framing our thoughts in Ryterski's words, might also remind (would it did the poet) of a tendency toward excessive self-critique rather than fair acknowledgement of achievement:

> Sure, I won those awards on the wall alright, but there's nothing to celebrate since
> They're a constant reminder of how things could have been compared to right now

This poem subsequently features a lightning-flash in technique: an extraordinary double-exposure (the Japanese term it *Kake-katoba*), whereby an adverb transitions "before" one's eyes:

> Room for the bright colors of the fabric to fill up the empty space on the wall before
> You knew it, you were taking down notes about what can stay and what needs to go

In The Beginning

I try to think of who the very first person was, but for every person that has existed
There is another person that has come before them so no one will ever know who
The original first person was because even the original first has an ancestor, correct
It is thought socially and in text that Adam and Eve were the original first people here
But remember where Adam and Eve came from, they came from someone else's life
Even so, there must have been someone who was truly independent from being born
Someone who didn't need anything or anyone in order to exist, but still just a person
In the beginning, there was one person who must have started it all; from then to now

There was one person who started it all, starpower swirling in between their palms
There was one person who had the whole universe in the palms of their hands and
What did they do with it? Their precious creation, their brainchild, their masterpiece
The person who held the whole universe in their hands was so kind to give it to us
Us, who the person with the universe in their hands may or may not have wanted
The best; only the finest for the ones who will live and die under your rule of thumb
There was one person who started it all who does not know who we are yet knows
Us, how we will rise and fall and how both of us will have an impact on each other

Whoever they are, I want desperately to be like them, to live and to love like they do
To be a person who doesn't need anything or anyone to exist, but still just a person
And to have my own world in between my own hands like the maker of the universe
What starpower do I hold? What do I have to offer? Instead of holding the universe
I am standing on shaky ground that isn't mine; I lack the confidence to own the earth
I find that most days I cannot gain control over the things that I want in life the most
And even now, I'm not exactly sure what exactly it is I want in and from life anymore
But I can write a poem or two, so that's where I find myself in my own tiny beginning

We, Who Walked Beneath The Stars

There was a place, and another place, and another and another
I never know what day and time it is, but they disappear regardless
There's a potted plant here, some fabric lying about messily there
I sat at my desk with my elbows on the table propping up my head
I was looking for something that was absent but had been set down
I knew for a fact that the thing was lying around here somewhere
And then that moment led to this moment and another and another
All of the dominos took their places as they did their signature move
The seasons changed over and over again and we trudged through
What was on the ground at the time, but we have not changed at all

And where do you think we're going? The most important question
Footsteps lead to footsteps; there's heavy breathing without stopping
Who you are, where you come from, and where you are going are
The most important questions you can ask yourself, I am told
So tell me, where are we going? Around the world? Or just here?
We are going to wherever our feet take us, wherever that place is
First to one place, then another place, and another and another
Regardless of whether our feet or our heads decide, we are moving
Moving towards somewhere beneath the starry starry night

When the night comes, there are dreams and more dreams
There are dreams of happy things, sad things, and scary things
And in the morning, when we wake up, the world is the very same
The world is identical to how it was before we went to sleep
There's a sky here and there's a ground there and stuff in between
And so we get up and continue walking where our feet guide us
And then one day leads to another day and another and another
Like trying to hold sand, the time slips out from between our fingers

What exactly are we doing with our lives again? We are walking
Through time, but only for the mere sake of existing as ourselves
What are we doing? We should have our act together by now
There are mistakes, and there are excuses, and there's also
A need to step out into what needs to be seen and done
But we, who walked beneath the stars, have not taken any
Real, meaningful steps, not for ourselves or for anyone else

Even though my steps are virtually useless, I can't help that
One step leads to another step, and another and another
My body moves forwards, and forwards, and forwards again
There's a body that is moving, and a face that exists, and hands
I look down at these hands and wonder whose hands these are
And I wonder what they're doing here and what they're made of
The majority of people are made of flesh and bone, but just maybe
The people around me are made of clay, like the Terracotta Warriors
The Terracotta Warriors stand guard over a precious thing that sleeps
Because it's the question of when, not if, their precious thing wakes up
May our footsteps be light as we walk past that sleeping potential

Of all the places we've been and all of the steps that we've taken
It still feels like we're taking the first step; we try to remember when
We took the first step, but for every step one takes there is another
Someone took before, so we'll never know who took the original first
We, who walked beneath the stars, know that the world is old
And because of its age, the world is just as exhausted as we are
And despite its age, the world is just as clueless as we are now
Both the world and us are spinning; take that how you want to
Perhaps today will be the day that you will walk amongst the dust

These Hands

I sat at my desk with my elbows on the table propping up my head
I looked down at my hands, taking them away from my chin and then
Turning them palms towards and away from my face, scanning them
For the veins and lines that proved that I existed as a human being
After staring at them for a while, I began to wonder who these hands
Really belonged to, what they were made of, and what they could do
Because it's a really funny thing how these hands came into existence

I was born with these hands, but they weren't the way they are now
The infant's fist has a death grip on the finger the mother put there
As I grew, my hands grew with me, but they didn't quite fully develop
Palms pressed together, my hand is a tiny little paw compared to my
Father's hands or my mother's hands, or anyone else's who's older
In comparison, I have much smaller hands that can't hold as much
What do you think that says about what I have to offer to the world?

It's funny how your hands can do so much and so little simultaneously
My hands can help me type this poem and drink my third cup of coffee
They can help me carry my things and shove favorite foods into my face
But when push comes to shove, I can't seem to get my hands dirty with
The meaningful, impactful work that really needs to be done in the world
Why can't I get my hands to toil? Do I not control them? My motor skills
Have been stunted, leaving me with what? What can I do with them now?

When you grow older, your hands are supposed to grow with you in time
But these hands on my wrists are done growing; they'll never fully develop
I'll grow old, and the skin on these hands will be dry, cracked, and wrinkly
They'll be worn alright, but not worn in the right way from supporting others
I'll have lived a life not worth living, and then what? What'll they make of me?
What will they make of me? Will they cut me up? Will they scratch my skin?
But for what it's worth, I can't bring myself to chop off these stupid hands

Doppelgänger Inside My Bedroom Mirror

There's a person inside of my bedroom mirror that looks like me but isn't me
They have the same straight brown hair, the same blue eyes, the same nose
There's a body that's moving, a face that exists, and they also have hands
The very same body and face and hands reflected for my personal horror
They can smile like me, they can cry like me, and they can talk like I can but
They're not me, there's no way in hell that this person in the mirror can be me
Who is this person who stands in the mirror before me? How did they get here?
There appears that there is a doppelganger inside of my bedroom mirror today

"To hell with this," I think as I abandon my reflection, "I'm done with this fuckery"
I clench my fists and punch my way around at the thought of what I have seen
Even when I turn away, I can't help but remember the look of that person's face
With that straight face and those sunken eyes, I don't want that person to be me
But there they are, in every mirror, in every window, and now in my memory too
"How dare they," I think, "how dare they make me feel the things I don't want to"
And to make matters worse, I don't know if there is a way to kill a doppelganger
"What kind of mess have I gotten into?," I think. "And what should I do for now?"

I told my therapist at the time about how there's a doppelganger following me
"What if the doppelganger is trying to help you in some way?," they asked
"I don't think so. If they were trying to help me, they wouldn't cause me pain."
"Well, Ray, sometimes the parts of us that cause us pain are trying to help us,
But somehow go too far. Maybe this part of you just went too far in helping you."
I stand my ground. "No," I say, "because this isn't a part of me. It can't be…."
"Ok, Ray. I didn't mean to upset you. I'm just trying to brainstorm with you."
I don't see that therapist anymore, and I wonder if that's for the best or not

I've managed to get by with no mirrors in my room, but they're still inside of me
"And where do you think you're going?" The doppelganger says in a taunting tone
"I'm going to get away from you," I swear to myself and the doppelganger in reply
The doppelganger laughs. "You'll never get away from me because I'm part of you"
I hope they're wrong. I don't want it to be right. I don't want that thing to be me.
I don't know if what it just said is right or wrong because there's a 50% chance
So when you see me in the real world, who do you see walking around as me?
Is who you see the real me, or is the person you see the person from the mirror?

Wall Decor

The room that I occupy in my parents' house is decorated how it's been for years
There's a map here, and a photo collage and several accolades hanging about there
Sure, I won those awards on the wall alright, but there's nothing to celebrate since
They're a constant reminder of how things could have been compared to right now
I could have won more of those awards if I wanted to, but instead, look at me now
I am a sad excuse of a human being that chooses to feel sorry for themselves when
There is no excuse for making lame excuses as to why you can't get your act right
Your act, that can't be held up, like the tye dye tapestry that commands strips falter
You smile and pretend to be happy, but you're not fooling anyone with that action

My mind thinks back to the tapestry that I had hanging in the university dorm room
My pride flag tapestry is packed up in a box, not to be used until there is room for it
Room for the bright colors of the fabric to fill up the empty space on the wall before
You knew it, you were taking down notes about what can stay and what needs to go
Along with all of the other things that I had set aside to use in my university's dorms
There are lots of things that will probably never see the light hanging overhead again
Along with my packed up belongings occupying the basement storage room shelving
There's a lot of things that have been forgotten and are collecting dust in my memory
But what I haven't forgotten about is leaving a place where I could have been well

I can't help but think back on the days where my being was in much better condition
But I'm not there, I thought. I'm here, not there. I'm here but I'm not there. Oh fuck.
You see what I'm getting at, right? The duality of my existence in space and in spirit
I'm in a weird spot here; I'm in a place where I can and cannot say that I really exist
Sure, I'm still human alright, and you can see and talk and interact with me anytime

But just merely occupying space and time isn't enough for me; you must see me for
I'm afraid that I'm hidden because I haven't done anything worthy of impressioning
The things that I touch with my fingers; I can still put my fingerprints on an object,
But it doesn't leave an actual mark; the empty space stares back at me in its triumph

Rumor has it that the empty spaces on those walls are there to stay for the long haul
It pains me to say that I don't think I'll ever go back again to where I once had been
Sure, I could always go back to school if I wanted to, but about that special time, no
Everyone has a special place that they want to go back to, somewhere fond of theirs
But for me, I don't miss any particular place, rather I miss a time I cannot go back to
No matter how hard I try, I can never go back to the time where I was actually to par
When the display at large is at large, there is a pain that paints the unknown distance
Everyone has to part with something at one point, but that doesn't mean it's painless
And my particular pain is the pain of life being painful when it shouldn't be painful

I've still got them, all of the things that I've always wanted to put on the walls and
I've still got it, the urge to make the space in the world that I occupy more beautiful
But what I don't have is the urge to step back and admire the colors and the scenery
I don't have the urge to admire my surroundings not because they don't matter but
Rather the colors and patterns that line the world's walls are just there for relaxation
They can help you think and feel but you have to do all of those things on your own
And since the colors and scenery are just that, they have no real power or influence
So the writing on the wall tells me that I should be proud of myself, but the thing is
I think that these words are mistaken because there's nothing for me to be proud of.

Unopened Doll

I can't open this box, the box of the doll my mom gave me as a Christmas present
When I hold it to my chest, I want so dearly to open it, but I must remind myself of
How I must keep myself disciplined and how it will last longer if I leave it unopened
So back in its spot on the bookshelf it goes until the next time I feel the urgent desire
I guess today must be the day that she must stand amongst the dusty shelves that need
So desperately to be cleaned, so desperate am I to put off the action of which I dread
So for now, she stands and watches patiently, and you'd think I'd be scared of this but
I'm not scared of dolls themselves; rather, I'm afraid of people comparing me to dolls

I'm afraid that when you compare me to a doll, you're saying that I'm built like one
There once was a time where I wanted people to tell me that I was as pretty as a doll
I would look at all of the women around me and wonder why I couldn't be like them
And to make matters worse, my parents saw me not as a doll but as an animal figurine
I'm still not comfortable with myself now, but I know now that it doesn't matter how
Awful myself or others can be or look, what matters is that I wasn't as fragile as dolls
I told myself that I would be strong and not be like porcelain, and here we are today

We've made quite a bit of progress though; I wouldn't be able to do that when young
My younger self isn't that far away; it seems like yesterday that I played with Barbies
At one point, I had at least a dozen dolls with a house and a pool and a couple of cars
That is, until I grew older and decided I would donate the toys I no longer played with
But those dolls, unless if something has happened to them, are still out there anywhere

They might not be played with anymore, but someone somewhere probably has them
Wherever they are and whatever condition they are in, those dolls are still and in tact
So for as long as they continue to exist, they'll still have everything they came with

And that's kinda how we are now, isn't it? We have our family, our house, our stuff
Except no one is supposed to play with us, at least that's true for the most of the time
Until someone comes along and decides to make you their doll and play your heart
To toy with your mind and make it so that you are dependent on them, so much so
That might remind you of old cliches, of hearts that are fiddles and marionette men
We don't forget the image of a puppet on a string, but let's also not forget the image
You might have heard that being a puppet on a string makes you inferior, a pushover
But for the person behind the puppet holding the strings, what does that make them?

Sometimes, I want to open the throats of the authorities that keep me inside this box
Call me whatever you want, but I'm telling you, my gut tells me I'd be much better
If I did what it tells me, and I've done everything everyone's told me…I don't know
They want me to be docile, to sit still and to shut up, but I want out from where I am
And when they put me on the stand, when they sentence me, I can say with credence
That I am innocent; I did nothing, but the doll, Doll Face, she did everything you say
But we cannot open the box, no, because those thoughts are best left as a keepsake so
No wonder people are afraid of dolls; you never know whether they are really empty

Terracotta

Terracotta clay for the pots and the bowls and plates that you'll use almost every day
They don't make pots and plates like they did back then, back during the Bronze Age
Under normal circumstances, this should be a good thing but I can't help but protest
My humiliation over my country's modern production value boils when I mull over
Where we went wrong from the time where we were making things from two hands
Now, I obviously wasn't alive during the Bronze Age, so maybe I shouldn't complain
But did it start then, or did we do ourselves in before we ever debuted on this earth?
I try to think of where we could have gone wrong, but for every scenario, there is an
Other scenario that could have come before, so we'll never be able to place a blame
So in fact, no one will ever know what it was really like back during the Bronze Age

In fact, no one today will ever know the struggles of our ancestors from that period
All we have are the remnants that were found of what our ancestors left us to study
You know, they found a bunch of terracotta statues in China one day, just by chance
A farmer was digging a hole in his field or something when he found what would be
The thing that you read about in the textbook for social studies when you were young
Terracotta Warriors, they called them, standing hundreds strong underneath the earth
Constructed without a choice, used without consent and without any hope of a reward
Perhaps they had something to be proud of, or maybe they couldn't leave one another
Whatever they stand for, they have their obligations and we have our own tasks about
Us, who dream of shaking hands with the people who passed on their dreams to us all

The Terracotta Warriors stand guard over a precious thing, one they love, that sleeps
Because it's a matter of who watches over and guards the dreams of the beloved ones
The dreams of their loved ones are lost to us today now that we have our own dreams
Dreams that might not be too different from the dreams those statues once had viewed
Dreams that we might have made come true in the time that keeps the distance between
Us, who stand looking at the statues and the statues themselves, staring back at us all
And in the end they still stand where they were discovered, and let us keep it that way
What moves them should be their own convictions, not the hands of ignorant moderns
Let us not touch them but let them touch us, and help inspire the dreams of the future
And what moves the world should be the individuals who do their part, and as for me?

As for me though, I didn't break ground at all on my walk; just the same old cemetery
I haven't done anything groundbreaking in school, at home, or anywhere as in general
So much so that I have stopped taking these stupid walks for my stupid mental health
And so much so that I've stopped doing these stupid tasks for these stupid checkpoints
On one hand, I can't move forward, and on the other hand, I can't wait or stand still as
Those Terracotta Warriors, what exactly are they waiting for? If they are waiting at all
Could it be that they're like me, wanting dearly to move forward but just not able to?
Or could it be the other way around - me like them, standing guard over the motion of
The emotions, cares, worries, and dreams of the people moving towards their futures?
It could be - no, it should be - that I too, am a special kind of Terracotta Warrior today

Rest Your Mind

"Good evening, Ray," I tell myself as I look into the mirror. I pay no attention to it
My tired expression says it's time for bed, and having made all the correct motions
I turn off the small lamp to the right of the mirror that was glowing ever so delicate
"Hmph," I sigh heavily then climb into bed, not knowing if I'll be able to rest today
The process of resting my mind is a complicated one, I think as I lay flat as a board
"If only I could get it to work one of these days," is what I'm thinking as my brain
Is resting on the pillow but really isn't resting at all; thoughts flow with the breaths
That make the oxygen course through my veins and into this big, complicated head
"You need to rest that brilliant, beautiful head of yours," I can hear my body saying
So with each of the breaths that make the oxygen go, I close my eyes and let it flow

While my eyes are closed, I wonder if I can keep them that way tonight and I think
There's no need to open your eyes for now because the world is the same as always
Just to make sure, I do open them just for a second, and I'm right; it is all the same
As I had left it before I had closed my eyes; knowing this, I close my eyes and start
To let go of all of these thoughts that I've thought and all of these feelings I contain
Starting with my head, if everything starts in your head and works its way outwards
Then I need to at least relax my head so that the rest of my body may follow in suit
"That's it," I can hear my body saying to me as it surrenders to the wave of comfort
"And that's it," I think but don't think as I recognize that I am at the drop off point
The drop off point where my body and mind are so exposed, but not uncomfortably

The drop off point where it is time to step across the threshold that holds you back
And you can always go back if you want to, but why you would want to backtrack
It is up to you to decide what you want for yourself, but if you choose to progress,
You'll find that beyond this point, there is no point in slowing down your progress
Your progress towards what you've always wanted, nothing can stop it from there
That point where your mind is so exposed and open but yet the world can't access
The place where no one but you can tell you what you're like; I was looking for it
I was looking for the person who was absent but was laid down somewhere close
My core self, the ideal Ray, they're closer to me now than I'd previously thought
That Ray that I can't reach when I'm awake, they're with me in my subconscious

That Ray that I can't reach when I'm awake, they beckon me further into the depths
Of my unconscious mind, I can hear it saying "just let go and let me help you out"
I let the other Ray take control and let them take me where they wanted to lead me
As I lose control, I can feel myself getting closer to the center of my subconscious
I listen to the sound that isn't there that I can hear without actually listening to and
If I pay attention without paying attention, I can feel my consciousness gently drift
And if I pay attention without paying attention, eventually sleep will come towards
A nice stopping point to let the hours slip by and watch the visions dance inside me
So yeah, eventually I'll fall asleep and then wake up to another day, but I won't rest
No, I won't get any rest until the day when I wake up and things are never the same

To The Place Where The Black Sea Ends

Little tugboat, where are you headed towards? Around the world? Or just here?
There was a place, and another place, and another and another and another place
The world whizzed by on all sides and there were colors; oh, how the colors made
A vibrant scene as we left the place we once knew, New World no longer knew
Its place in the world, distraught by the thought of city or country not upon any hill
Hill that we fell from; my place in the world is fragile, so much that I'll settle for any
Any old hill will do; the Old World being both the Old World and the New World and
As for the New World? The Old World stretches before and behind me in new ways
I can't see it, the place where I wanted to be; it's like we're in the middle of the sea

The Black Sea, bordered by Ukraine, Turkey, and Russia, isn't really black, is it?
But I bet you it spans out in front and behind you for miles and miles and miles and
Well, you can get lost easily in a place like that even if you have a compass on you
I get lost in my thoughts and feelings like that quite often; I lose my sense of reason
Life's compass, your morality and reason, points the way to where you should head
I know where my life should be headed towards, but we're nowhere near where we
Won't be confused by the lack of guidance and support from the broken compassion
Won't compose the water on and off my face and won't compose my confused state
Want to be somewhere pleasant but simultaneously don't know if it's what I want now

Want to be somewhere pleasant but simultaneously doubt whether it's what I want
That's what I wanted when I started my journey, but now I'm not so sure of myself
Where I started this journey, I had to start somewhere, but now I've forgotten here
I've forgotten why I started this journey and I've forgotten what I wanted from it all
I think that I was thinking I wanted to say goodbye to something when I started on

This journey, the one I'm now sick and tired of being on, has left me feeling sick to
My stomach is full of knots and my head is empty; I just can't put my fingers on it
 "And do I even want out of this confusion?," I think to myself, writing in my journal
These feelings that have me in a mess, I can't just simply adjourn them into orders

But there's no order to the sea, is there? It's put together into one big, sloppy mess
I can't order the sea to take a different form, and I can't order my thoughts to align
The shore makes a line and the rest follows; why I can't make myself more like that
I don't know; I don't know anything anymore, and it sinks my spirits down to its seat
The bottom of the Black Sea, it could be black after all 'cause the light cannot reach
The light that makes light bulbs shine in your mind can't reach up where it should be
Your brain lights up with synapses when it wants to think but they just can't connect
To make the thoughts in your brain work like they should, everything has to be right
So I know something isn't right with me because nothing is like it is supposed to be

And there's nothing wrong with that, there's nothing technically wrong with me now
But since my brain isn't working like it should, there's nothing really right here either
So I'm here, stuck in the middle of the ocean with my boat and my broken compass
We're here because we're here and it's going to stay this way for a little longer now
And that's fine; I'm in it for the long haul, and I'll stay here for as long as I needed it
And when the confusion passes, when my brain begins to function the way it must,
I know that I'll be able to go on my way one of these days; it's just a matter of time
And for those of you who are the way I am, for the others stranded out in the ocean
The Black Sea might seem bleak right now, but I promise there's a place at its end

Somewhere, Anywhere, A Train Runs Through It

Curled up in a fetal position in bed, I listen to noises from the outdoors
From my window, I can hear the sound of a train whistle; a train goes by
There's a train, and another train, and another and another; they all pass
The sound of the whistle makes a musical interval that I cannot identify,
But curled up into a fetal position in bed, I listen quietly to the music that
Makes its way from one end of town to the other and then beyond towns
I've never actually seen train tracks anywhere in this small, sleepy town
But they are out there somewhere; the trains exist out there somewhere
I don't know exactly where that is, but somewhere, a train runs through it

I can picture it in my imagination, a train runs sturdy and tall through the
Empty tracks that run through the night, the wind rushes all around after
The sleek beast that pushes its way forward with the strength of passion
Passion and energy that has withstood the test of time, the train travels
Towards both its destination and the future; there'll be trains in the future
They'll be there for sure because they've made it this far already and the
Wheels that turn have momentum; momentum that keeps on keeping on
Where that energy, that strength, comes from I don't know but anywhere
Somewhere, anywhere, a train will run through it; I know this for certain

I've ridden the MetroLink before, but not a proper locomotive as I detail
But I've stepped onto one that was no longer in use when I was young
My memory of this is very vague, but I remember how big the thing was
And me, so small in comparison; what am I in comparison to this beast?

Do I even begin to live up to the legacy of the locomotives of our past or
Do I even begin to scrape the surface of what they have done for us all?
I believe not to be as resilient, reliable, or hard-working as they had been
And I believe that I don't even begin to compare to what they were and
I believe that I don't deserve such a cherished remembrance as theirs

But there's got to be something that they don't have, something missing
Why would they go the distance if this were not the case? I'm not certain
Their shining example might not last as long as they themselves will last
You can put the pedal to the metal as much as you want but it'll still rust
No matter what you do, where you go, or whatever you see, you cannot
Make time stop in its tracks; barreling down at you like a speeding train
So no matter where you go, what you see, or what you do, take the time
To bite the bullet, let the lead take its course, and make every turn count
Through a time, somewhere, anywhere, a train will run through its course

So you're not as shiny and beautiful as you once had been but so what?
Like a train, you've been keeping on keeping on, and that's so admirable
It's just a little bit of rust and a few spots where the paint is chipped is all
It doesn't actually hurt, does it? And it doesn't make you broken, correct?
If you can still do the same level of performance as always, I'd say it's ok
It's okay for you to have a few blemishes here and there, and it's alright
For me to make mistakes here and there as long as I keep on getting up
Sometimes we all have to compromise, and as for the train's conditions
These may be exhausted, somewhere, anywhere, a train runs through there

Day & Age, Sam's Town, & Me

Two CDs sit on a shelf and ask someone if they need help
They sing the tune with the words, the words I needed to hear
Actions speak louder than words, but songs speak even louder
So whenever I see those two CDs, I remember where I came from
So whenever I listen to those two CDs, I breathe in some dark nostalgia
The singer sings that he can get by fine; he just needs some time
Perhaps I can yet again apply some lyrics, like bandages, to the wounds

I got my first taste of Day & Age when I was in a very dark place
Sitting in that dark basement, I dared to listen to my sister's music
When I tuned into "Spaceman," there was something that drew me in
What I heard was that it is normal to dream about dark things like I did
Finally, there was someone who was like me, who danced with darkness
So instead of doing what needed to be done, I stuck around and listened
In "Losing Touch," "Neon Tiger," and "A Crippling Blow," I heard my struggle
And I understood then that the writers of the music wanted the best for me
That was the first time that anyone told me that I had value, so I was hooked

At the same time, I discovered Sam's Town, and grew to love it too
I grew to love the sound of loud, squealing guitars and loud drums
I held onto the words of "Sam's Town," "Bling," and "Uncle Johnny"
The riot of a record gave me a call to action that no one wanted to say

And the singer's conviction solidified the fact that I had to get better
No matter how much the sky mocked me, the music gave me strength
The music gave me strength to play the game of tug of war going on
Between the real me and the me that I thought that I was and still am

Listening to the artist's newer works, I'm not as into it as I once was
We've both changed so much, both the artist and myself; it's weird
Listening to their music now, it doesn't give me the same energy
I get the feeling that the power in the music I was drawn to is gone
Replaced by something more lackluster, appealing to the masses
So I stay away from their music because it lacks its genuinity
Not that the music has told me not to listen to it or anything like that
It's just that "Wonderful Wonderful" made me realize those songs
Were probably written for someone else, someone who isn't me

What happened all those years ago was kind of a weird situation
On one hand, music isn't made for the personal gain of others
On the other hand, I don't think the original artists would really mind
Speaking of which, if you are the original artist, and if you're reading,
Not only would I like to say thank you, but I also just have one question
All this time, I've believed in the you who has believed in me, so I thought
But since I know what I know now, is it time for us to find our own words?

Pavane Pour Une Infante Défunte

Bum, bum bum bum bum, bum bum bum bum bum; bum, bum bum bum bum, bum bum bum bum bum bum bum, bum bum bum bum bum bum bum, and etcetera, etc.
That's the opening to Maurice Ravel's "Pavane pour une infante defunte" for you
Regardless whether it's translated as "Pavane for a dead princess" or if it means
"Pavane for a dead infant," the title of the piece still doesn't mean anything to Ravel
The piece itself, according to Wikipedia, is not an actual tribute to a dead princess
Instead, Ravel wanted to write a song that a Spanish princess might have danced to
But even with these facts in mind, I still find my mind picturing a dead baby princess

I know, we all thought that the title of the piece was important to the music's meaning
I always thought this song was about an actual dead princess even though it is not
The baby girl lies still, not upset or crying, just peacefully asleep, not to be disturbed
She probably would have danced to this song in the ballroom if she had lived longer

But instead of dancing, those feet are never to be used, curled up with rigor mortis
The parents look down at their own feet, wondering what they did to deserve this act
Passing the girl's casket in the line of onlookers, let us not wake the girl by stomping
May our footsteps be light as we pass by this sleeping potential; potential ungrowing

And what became of the girl that wasn't also became of Ravel himself; so in the end
This piece could actually commemorate someone if you think of Ravel when listening
Poor Maurice, his brain slowly deteriorating; the shell of the man that he once was
He didn't know what his fate would be when he wrote "Pavane pour une infante…"
But when he wrote "Bolero," things had changed; the very first symptom presented
Not as a cough or sore throat or pain in the side, but a piece that outlasted composer
Along with the temporal lobe, the restrictions against what was allowed crumbled
To give you bum, bum bum bum bum, bum bum bum bum bum, etcetera etcetera

The Night We All Sang Together

When the night comes, there are dreams and more dreams; all sorts of dreams dance
Dreams of happy things, of sad things, and of scary things, they all dance to the beat
The beat and rhythm that your heart makes every night is a special kind of music the
Heart's beating is music to and in your ears that reminds you that you're a living you
Along with the pitch and melody of the expansion and contraction of your lung sacks
The body's music is in time with your consciousness so that others may tune into you
So every time you open your mouth to speak to another, it's music made just for them
But not now, because your eyes are dancing in REM; the deepest kind of sleep awaits
Awaiting me every night are dreams that dance, some of which I don't remember well
But there's the one that I couldn't possibly forget, the one that keeps evading my grasp

I wasn't actually there when it happened, but I swear it was all very real to me, indeed
There was you, who were under the dazzling lights; and there was me underneath you
There was you in your individual radiance and there was me engulfed in the audience
And for a moment I thought I could never be on the same level as you, but by miracle
One moment I was reaching out my hand towards yours and the next you had taken it
We stayed with our hands together; me not pulling you down and you not pulling me
Up where you are, I can't see myself; and down where I am, you can't see yourself as
Well, look what we have here; neither of us wants to make the first move, but in time,
We're going to have to break apart this tug of war that isn't a tug of war in due course
And you know what happened next? The real world ended up calling me back to earth

"Damnit," I thought as my eyes adjusted to the surrounding light through my windows
This had just been a dream; I'm still the same me that I was before I had gone to sleep
And it sucks that whenever I wake up again, I still have the same life that I did before
I can dream all I want, but only in my dreams can I get to the same level where you are
You're tucked away in your little pocket of the world and I'm stuck in my little pocket
And we'll probably never cross paths at all; our hands won't touch together in real life
But because I desire without hope, I keep dreaming of the night that it won't be fiction
I dream of being able to emerge from the crowd, that dark space where I'm not special
I dream of one day being of the same level as you so that you are no longer above me;
And I dream of showing off my own radiance to others: my time, talents, and treasure

So I dream over and over again of hearing you in the flesh and sharing the sacred song
It's a funny little dream, but it's my dream; there's no way I'm going to stop chasing it
Because I don't think it's fair that you're the only one of us that is deemed exceptional
And I know the dream probably won't come true; I'm always the same me I have been
But it doesn't hurt to dream of something better for yourself sometimes when you feel
Like it, when you feel like you're not radiant or special, go ahead and have the dream
And when you dream nice dreams, you'll be alright even though you're still the same
As for me, I will still be the same, but I have this nice dream; when things will change
When you come back to town, when you say that you love us again, that'll be the day
And when the right moment arrives, I will open my mouth and let the melody fall out

What We Must Do

Before I left the university campus I used to attend, one of my favorite things about
The place was this giant Roman fountain in the middle of campus, "The Colonnade"
I would go there at odd hours of the morning to watch the pretty lights and question
What I was doing there, I don't exactly know; and I still don't have the answers they
Didn't know it at the time, and still don't know that I'd be stuck with the same query
And I still don't have the answers to the questions the former me was asking of them
It's because as I go through my life today as the present me, I'm still asking the same
What exactly am I doing with my life again? What am I supposed to do with myself?
What I can't help but keep focusing on is the fact that I haven't really done anything
So what is the answer? When will I figure my act out? How will I move on with life?

What am I doing with my life again? What are we doing here? It's a valid question
Since most people know the answer to that question for themselves, I feel I should
But I don't, do I? What do you think that makes me? So what does it make of me?
Ok, so I do know the answers to those questions; not knowing makes me feel tiny
It's like I'm a kitten who is trying to go up a staircase for the first time in their life

I can't get a grip onto the next step I'm supposed to take towards a better existence
And it's all because I don't know the very basics, the foundations, of my existence
Ok, so maybe that's a bit of a harsh statement, but I can't ignore what is remaining
What's remaining when it is all said and done, I know the answer to that question
At the end of the day, there is me and all of my flaws laid out for everyone to view

There are mistakes, and there are excuses, and then there is the need to step out into
What needs to be seen and done at the time, I can't seem to be able to figure that out
I know what I've been told to do, and I know what I should have done in the past but
What we must do in times like these, I don't know; I don't know, don't know, I don't
And maybe I don't have to know the answers because things are how things are then
If it is what it is, then maybe I should just accept that fact and move forward with life
Sure, I'll never have the answers that I want, and I'll never stop asking myself about
When I'll get to a point where I'm actually doing something with what I was given -
And I do know that I will get there; these things just take time - I'll know what to do
It's because now I think that what I must do, the universe will tell me what I must do

What We Haven't Fixed

Recently, I've had quite a bit of time to reflect on my life and where I should be next
Who I am, where I came from, and where I'm going, I'm asking the most important
Questions with no easy answers, the questions that I've been asking for a little while
And I've decided that the answers will come to me when the universe tells me them but
My flaws, my shortcomings, I can't help but see them when I look at my own frame
And when I take it all in, I can't help but notice that there's much we have not fixed
And because there's much that we haven't fixed, I'm prone to being negative
Because there's much we haven't fixed, I'm prone to thinking things that I'm broken
Among other things, I think and I think and I think about how I've not fixed myself
If only I had fixed myself earlier, I wouldn't be this broken, this bruised or battered

If only I had fixed everything needing it, I wouldn't be this broken, bruised, battered
But I guess that also works the other way around; if I wasn't bruised there'd be zero
Nothing to fix, no flaws, that's impossible; everyone has things needing to be fixed
And there's still time to do the inner work that needs to be done, but it's frustrating

To see myself this way, I think I need to see myself in a different way one more try
One more try towards the person that I want to be, and one more try to live truthful
Truthful to myself and truthful to my pocket of the world, I'm trying to consciously
Love myself and others and awaken the potential I hold and my sleeping core self
And when I wake up, maybe the world will still be the same before I went to sleep

But even if the world is still the same, I don't want to fall into that trap once again
It's because we're in the middle of the Great Awakening, and I have chosen a light
The universe is enlightening me with its wonders and splendors, and is calling me
I can feel it pulling me, beckoning, calling out to me to return to my rightful home
My home in the universe, my place at the foot of the spiral staircase to the galaxy
I stand now in between those asleep and those awakened, the alive and the asleep
The universe will tell me who I am, where I came from, and where I should head
And the universe and I will take care of what we haven't fixed because in the end
In the end, there will always be things we haven't fixed, but that's perfectly okay

Thinking Of You

Hey there, says the email I'm about to send. Hope you're doing the best you can.
And it's true, dear friend, I do hope you're doing the best that you possibly can do
Actually, no, I *know* that you're doing everything that you can to take care of things
But just for the heck of it, I start my emails off with these formalities for both of us
I start my emails off with these formalities so that the both of us know where to start
Starting from the day that we both met in person for the very first time in your office
I've had the pleasure of residing within your offices and have enjoyed your company
After all this time of being friends together, it really hasn't been all that long, right?
We've both shared so much with each other: thoughts and worries and so much else
In this exchange, I couldn't have asked for a better person to share everything with

No matter what I do, I can no longer sleep at night, and when I can't, I think of you
I always think about what would have happened if I hadn't met you at that university
If I had chosen to go to a different university, or even if I hadn't have changed majors
I don't know where we would be today if things had been any different, if we hadn't
Me - at the start of my career - and you - near the finish - met reading between lines
You - in your own little pocket of the world - and me - in my own separate pocket -
We communicate through lines that we write on our own, so we may have a way of
Taking away the spaces between our words takes space away from us and our texts
In this text, I would like to give you my word; a new word for the way ahead of us
We must take away the space between us and our thoughts and our worries or else

With all that out of the way, there's something I need to get out of the way mentally
When you say I'm terrific, there's something you're unknowingly not accounting for
Something that I've never told you about is the fact that I've lied to you in the before
I lied to you about reading Leskov, and I think I've lied about watching your lectures
I have lied to you since we first met in class, and I have lied to everyone before that
I'm trying to think of the first lie that I've ever told, but for every lie there's one more
There's always another lie that caused the one that's lying in front of your conscience
I think that I might be a bit of a compulsive liar, but I don't have a diagnosis for it yet
I think that there's something that's seriously wrong with me because I can't not lie to
Compensate for what I am lacking; I want to make things up to you somehow, honest

I know that you have some serious trust issues, so I think I know how you will feel
But I'm telling you this because I know it will help me get closer to telling the truth
I don't know if you'll still be my friend by the time you finish reading this, if you do
Finish it all with the pages where you want to leave off; leave off of this settlement
As this may never be truly settled, you have the right to feel whatever you desire to
You have the right to do whatever you feel is the right thing for your own wellth, so
If this friendship ends like I expect it to, like the previous ones - and yes, it will end -
I don't care about what went wrong or who said what to whom, or about who's right
At the end of the day, I care only about you, your wellbeing, and your way forward
So no matter what happens to us, please know that I will always be thinking of you

All That Have Fallen

All that have fallen have taken their places amongst the stars above
We wish them the best as we see them above and us stuck on Earth
Us stuck on Earth and them up above; those who have fallen and we
We, who made the best of things, and they, who fell in their struggle
We, who still feel the pain that befell onto them, and they who have
Given their pain, we chalk it up to be that falling was not a decision
And they're fine now that they've passed on their grief, it's just that
All of the dominos took their places as they did their signature move
So they're alright alright, but it's what befell them that made them fall
Just like the pain that we feel now is at fault for our own trial and error
So now that we here on Earth have their pain, are we really different?

I don't think we're really all that different really; just better with coping
At the base of the spiral staircase, I could see the lights of the fallen
And I took the very first step towards my peers, but couldn't get there
I didn't get past the first step because we're similar but not the same
I am not like you, and you are not like me, and we are not like them,
And I live in my body, and you in your body, and they in their bodies
Everybody has their own body, one that is their own and theirs alone
And everyone has their own consciousness, one that is not tradable
So that's why I can't get to where I want because we can't trade ours
Because we can't trade consciousnesses, I can't trade places with you
And because we can't trade souls, you can't trade places with me too

The way I am now, and the way you are now; I'm not sure we'd want
To give up our places in the world for each other, but it's just what it is
I shouldn't resign myself; no, I shouldn't settle, and neither should you
Please don't settle for anything less than what you do indeed deserve
And you do deserve so much love for the love that you put to the test
Because you love me, and I love you, and they all love each other so
Much love and much pain have made you the way you are right now
And much love and much pain has made me the way I am right now
And the same goes for the fallen, those who are here but also astray
Much love and much pain has made us the way we are but it will not
Change the fact that we are who we are and we are where we are at

Who we are and where we are at, our lives are separate but together
When you can't sleep at night, reach upwards and try to shake hands
With the flawed people that made you the person who you are today
They wish you the best as they see you stuck here struggling on Earth
Struggling here on Earth, we may be like them, but we are so different
Because we have a choice in the matter, let's try to keep our balances
Struggling here on Earth, let's do our best to avoid the place they fell to
I make the best of what I have, and you make the best of what you get
We all make the best of what we have, and we strive to do our best for
The fallen remind us of who we are and where we could have been but
All that have fallen are still capable of making the best of what they get

Face The Curtain

"What am I going to do with myself," I asked to the white curtains on my window
I spend a lot of my time nowadays just staring at the closed window, blinds drawn
Ever since I dropped out of school, I've spent a lot of my time like this, just staring
At those stupid curtains; how dare they be so clean, so pure, so unlike me: stainless
And then there's The Curtain, the one from the song I want played at my funeral
The Curtain, the one they sing about in "Always Look On The Bright Side of Life"
Can I? May I? I want to do what the song says, savor the last moments of my time
But every time I've tried to write the note, conjure the will, I just can't do the deed
I've prepared and revised my preparations over and over again, but here I am, alive
I can't kill myself for the life of me; for the life of me, something's holding me back

No matter how hard I try, I can't seem to be able to kill myself; I don't understand it
You might think that it's a good problem to have, but it's a problem for me because
Because I think I'm a broken machine that needs to be thrown away with the refuse,
The fact that I can't seem to throw myself away really bothers me; it's troubling me
What's troubling me more is that I know that if I do go through with it, it might hurt
It might hurt you more than it hurts me, and I don't want to hurt anyone but myself
So what do I do? Is it okay to be a coward? Trust me, I'd love to stay here with you
But not killing myself might hurt too because that pains me more than it pains you;
I'm in this tug of war between what'll make me happy and what'll make you happy
And maybe killing myself isn't the thing that'll make me happy, but what else will?

About that, I've always thought that making you happy is what will make me happy
And maybe killing myself isn't the thing that'll make you happy, but what else will?
Actually, I know that killing myself won't make you happy but nothing else ever has
Nothing that I have ever done has ever made anyone happy, so there's no meaning in
Going to school, going to meet up with people, or going anywhere & doing it all over
Over and over again, I get up, do my routine, and go to bed again just like a robot can
Go through the steps that are programmed into them and live out your life on autopilot
It's gotten me nothing, taken me nowhere, this lifestyle that's with and without feeling
But maybe it's better than dying; killing myself isn't going to get me anywhere either
So I don't know what I'm going to do with myself; I've thought all that I could have

Now, I think that if I could just have love from someone, if someone could say it's ok
Maybe I'd be alright if a kind, gentle, and loving person were to comfort me just a bit
A support system, I think it's called; one that I can actually rely on without much pain
I think that I'm going to get up, go through my routine, and give love to other people
And I do think that love is the answer; it's just that love isn't a thing that comes easily
Actually, love does come easily; it's the changes that love makes that isn't that simple
Maybe things will never change; I might not be able to give up my adolescent anxiety
I might not know what to do with myself, but I do know what I will do when it comes
To you, I will love you for as long as I live; it is because love is what makes us living
So even if something bad happens to me, I will live on in the love that I've given you

In The Apocalypse

Nobody knew we were in the apocalypse until even the dust had vanished from us all
In the media, they show the apocalypse as some big to do, but that is not how it went
One moment, everything was the way we had left it the day before and then the next,
Poof! Everything and everyone you've ever loved just vanished with a snap of fingers
It was like watching the sand in an hourglass make its way from the top to the bottom
One moment, you're looking at the sand at the top of the timepiece, watching it trickle
And then the next, you see the sand at the bottom of the timepiece, and you're puzzled
"What the? How did that happen?," is what you're thinking; you didn't see it coming
And neither did we; the apocalypse just sort of snuck up on us from behind, and poof!

Poof! In the blink of an eye, the world just silently slipped out of existence; great, huh
I guess the world really is gone for good, huh; well, that's quite the problem, isn't it?
No more houses or schools or businesses and no more people to occupy the buildings
And if there's no more people, then there is no more life, happiness, and joy, no more
Of anything I had cherished, I think I'm going to miss having you at my side the most
No more pretty face, no more gentle smile, and no more mild nature; no more of what
Makes you special, the way you do the things you do; and how you like what you like
You like what you like and I like what I like; and we don't adore what we don't adore
And you know what I don't adore? I don't like how everything I loved had to leave me

Why did the world have to leave us like that? And why did you have to leave with it?
I want you back; I want the world back; I want everything and everyone I loved back
But I cannot have that, can I? None of those things or people are going to come back
Because I don't have the power to bring back what I loved even if they could go back
Back in the world, there's nothing for them to come back to even if they desired to be

What they used to be, what the world used to be, if only the past could see the present
For what it's worth, I am grateful that I got to live and breathe with those who passed
Through the veil, where the future isn't the future and time isn't time, I could've gone
But instead, I am where I am; and I think how it could be different, but here is where

Here is where, in the end of the end; and no matter how hard I try, that won't change
And I was looking for the rubble that wasn't there but I knew had been put someplace
But the shrapnel that was supposed to be there wasn't there; it is as if it never existed
Looking at the solar system now, you could never be able to tell that there had been
A planet between Venus and Mars that spun and danced along with all the other stars
That body of matter and heat that housed so much life without having a life of its own
We must say goodbye to where we once called home since the universe wished us out
Out where there is not even nothing, I'll come and find you if you're still who you are
But it's okay if you're not because it's not your fault and I still love you, living or dead

Of course I still love you; you and your essence, you and your quirks and your nature
I love you and everything about you; that's the one thing the end time can't take away
Because it's the one thing I've got a grip on after everything else vanished from sight
And as long as I remember what it was like before the end, everyone will still be here
And as long as I remember what it was like to have everything the way it was, it'll be
The way it was in my mind, there was so much love and life in the world that existed
And it still exists, here in my heart as long as I keep the memory alive; safe & sound
And when it's all over, when I'm finally not alone anymore, I'll tell you of the fables
How even in the apocalypse, there's no such thing as total annihilation and disrepair
Because in the apocalypse, there was one person; there was one person who had love

We, Who Stood Upon The Earth

I said that today would be the day you'd stand amongst the dust, and I was right and wrong
Because after everything vanished, there is no dust to speak of or walk on or stand amongst

You don't believe me because in your world, everything is the way it was before it collapsed
Sure, your world has its problems, but everything in your world is where it has always been
But believe you're going to have that comfort ripped away from you one day; it will happen

"Everyone is going to die someday," the people who once existed kept on insisting at us all
At the time, it was annoying, but as annoying as it was to hear, they were right in their words
With the snap of a finger, everything and everyone I had ever loved was ripped away from me
Like trying to hold sand, the world just slipped out of existence without anyone on it noticing

And without me even noticing, I lost my grip on myself and slipped out of existence alongside
Alongside with the rest of my peers, the world killed me, reduced me to just a lonely specter
I'm just a lonely ghost with Nowhere to go, nowhere to call home; but I feel nothing because
Well, I'd say that I felt something, but you have to have more than just a soul for you to say so
Because we, who stood upon the Earth, are the ones who gave up those feelings when we left

At least we were supposed to give up those feelings when we left, but I might have kept some
I probably wouldn't feel so confused if I had left the feelings behind like I was supposed to or
Maybe it doesn't matter; well, oh well, I didn't do what I was supposed to well yet I am well
At least I think I'm well; I can't quite explain it to you - not well spoken - but yeah, I'm well
I'm not very well spoken, so perhaps well isn't the right word; but, I'll tell you that I'm well
And there's a lot more that I want to tell you, but I can and can't tell you about it all because

We, who stood upon the Earth, are unsure of how we can be speaking to you without existing
At least I thought that I didn't exist anymore; it doesn't make sense to be the last one standing
I don't understand why I of all people was chosen to be the last one standing because I do not
Have any sort of special characteristics or powers, nor did I wish to be the last man standing

It was my wish to be with you no matter what happened, but magic and wishes are not reality
At least I thought that wishes and magic weren't reality, but I can't explain how else I got here
Here, my reality, I don't get any of it, but somehow I've survived, somehow I'm still aware of

Somehow, I've ended up in this alternate dimension, a space in between your and my world
On one side, I'm shut out from the destroyed remains of my world, and on the other side you
I can see you in your world on the other side, as if separated, shut out, by a transparent glass
I don't know if you can actually hear me through the glass, but I am talking to you, you know
And you know, even if you can't actually hear me, you can still try to make an effort to listen
Unless if what I'm saying to you isn't worth your time, unless if my words aren't important;
Well, regardless of whether listening to the words of the past are important or not, listen still
Because when what happened to me happens to you, you're going to wish that you did listen

What I think is that you're listening to me, but you're also not listening to me, and that's fine
I know that my words don't fall on deaf ears, but ones that spew them out from the other side
I blame the glass that stands between us for this; the space that separates us from one another
I don't like it, but it's there for a reason; we can't stand on the same ground since, you know,
You know, I'm itching for a sweet old fashioned on the rocks, but I can't knock down a glass
I can't knock down a glass of alcohol, and I can't knock down the glass wall separating us
But what I'm trying to say is that my words, whether you listen or not, break down the glass
And what I'm trying to say is that it doesn't matter if you're listening because talking helps
And what I'm trying to say to myself is that I can still talk to you no matter what happened

Okay, so say that I might have triumphed over the end of all ends; that's fine and all, but now,
Now what am I supposed to do? So yeah, I triumphed, but not because of any special powers
I'm still the same me that I was before this all happened, just without the parts that make me
Like you, I once had a heart and a soul; I am but I'm not just like you are, a loving individual
That's probably the reason why I haven't died just yet, I think, because I still have love in my
Nonexistent heart and soul, the hearts and souls that were lost in the end live on in love, and
I may have lost everything mortal about me, but I still have the love that I once saved for you
You in your world, and me in mine; both of our worlds still have an abundance of love there
And because love conquers the end, I'm sure you'll triumph over the apocalypse just like me
I can't tell you when it's going to happen to you, but when it does, maybe you'll be with me